Short Stories for Students, Volume 47

Project Editor: Kristen A. Dorsch

Rights Acquisition and Management: Ashley Maynard and Carissa Poweleit Composition: Evi Abou-El-Seoud

Manufacturing: Rita Wimberley Imaging: John Watkins © 2018 Gale, A Cengage Company

Since this page cannot legibly accommodate all

Gale
27500 Drake Rd.
Farmington Hills, MI, 48331-3535

ISBN-13: 978-1-4103-2859-5
ISSN 1092-7735

This title is also available as an e-book.
ISBN-13: 978-1-5358-4557-1
ISBN-10: 1-5358-4557-1
Contact your Gale, A Cengage Company sales representative for ordering information.

Printed in Mexico
1 2 3 4 5 6 7 22 21 20 19 18

Printed in Mexico
1 2 3 4 5 6 7 22 21 20 19 18

Unaccustomed Earth

Jhumpa Lahiri

2008

Introduction

In a 2013 interview with the *New York Times*, the Bengali American author Jhumpa Lahiri takes exception to the literary category immigrant fiction:

> I don't know what to make of the term.... If certain books are to be termed immigrant fiction, what do we call the rest? Native fiction? Puritan fiction? This distinction doesn't agree with me. Given the history of the United States, all American fiction could be classified

as immigrant fiction…. From the beginnings of literature, poets and writers have based their narratives on crossing borders, on wandering, on exile, on encounters beyond the familiar…. The tension between alienation and assimilation has always been a basic theme.

Though Lahiri herself might object to the label, most critics would class most of her books and short stories firmly in the genre. Her work illuminates the immigrant experience, exploring issues of identity, family, tradition, and acclimatization. Lahiri's "Unaccustomed Earth," the title story of her 2008 collection of the same name, is a prime example of her work, because it tackles these themes.

The story centers on Ruma and her retired, widowed father. When he comes for a weeklong visit, Ruma ponders whether to invite him to move in with her family. Her perceptibly strained marriage, her own discontent at her narrow role as a stay-at-home mother, and her unresolved grief over her mother's death all factor into her decision. Meanwhile, Ruma's father becomes acquainted with his young grandson and ponders whether he is content with his solitary existence.

Author Biography

Lahiri was born on July 11, 1967, in London, England, into a Bengali family originally from Calcutta. Her given name was Nilanjana Sudeshna Lahiri, but she chose to go by her family's nickname for her, Jhumpa. Her father was a university librarian, and her mother was a teacher.

When Lahiri was still very young, her family moved to Kingstown, Rhode Island. Though her parents strove to instill in their children a pride in their heritage and culture, Lahiri still felt like an outsider. She used writing as an outlet for her confused emotions and remembered working on stories during recess at elementary school.

Lahiri graduated from Barnard College in 1989 with a bachelor's degree in English literature. After earning three master's degrees at Boston University —in English, creative writing, and comparative literature and art—she continued her studies, completing a doctorate in Renaissance studies, also from Boston University. Lahiri briefly taught creative writing at Boston University and the Rhode Island School of Design, but throughout the 1990s while in graduate school, she wrote numerous short stories, publishing in prestigious magazines such as the *Harvard Review*, the *New Yorker*, and *Story Quarterly*. Nine of these stories were included in her first book, *Interpreter of Maladies*, which was published in 1999. The collection was awarded the

Pulitzer Prize for Fiction and several other major awards and led to Lahiri's being honored with a 2002 Guggenheim Fellowship.

Lahiri's 2003 novel *The Namesake* was adapted into a major motion picture in 2006. "Unaccustomed Earth" was published in a short-story collection of the same name in 2008. In 2013, Lahiri released *The Lowland*, which is about the choices of two brothers that lead them down very different paths in life. Never one to shy away from a challenge, Lahiri wrote her next book in Italian. *In altra parole* (2015) chronicles her struggle to learn the language through immersion. Also in 2015, Lahiri was awarded a National Humanities Medal by President Barack Obama. As of 2017, Lahiri lived in Brooklyn, New York, with her husband and two children.

Plot Summary

As "Unaccustomed Earth" begins, Ruma's father has lost his wife during a routine surgical procedure, has retired from his job, and has begun traveling, taking organized tours in Europe. While out of the country, he sends postcards to Ruma, but the messages are matter-of-fact rather than affectionate and personal. Before his next trip overseas, he is coming to Seattle to visit Ruma and her family.

While Ruma's father is visiting, her husband, Adam, is on a business trip. He travels often with his new job, which is the reason for their recent move from New York to Seattle. The move is a big change for Ruma, who has left her part-time work at a law firm and her friends in Brooklyn. But she is happy that Adam's high salary with the new position allows her to stay at home with Akash, their son, all day. She has struggled with leaving him since her mother's unexpected death of a reaction to a medicine during what should have been a simple surgical procedure.

With her father widowed and now retired, Ruma feels she should ask him to move in with them. Adam does not feel it is necessary but does not object. This highlights a cultural difference between husband and wife, for in her traditional Bengali American upbringing, such family closeness is more expected than in Adam's European American background. However, she fears that her father's presence will complicate their lives or that he will be a burden. Pregnant for the second time and in an unfamiliar city, Ruma is not content with her life.

As Ruma's father makes his way to her house, he recalls exhausting trips to India to visit family with his wife, Ruma, and Ruma's brother, Romi. This trip to Seattle is easy by comparison, with only himself and one bag to keep track of. His European tours are equally simple, and while with the tour group, he enjoys the companionship of a Bengali American widow named Mrs. Bagchi. She is very different from his late wife, wearing Western clothes and teaching statistics at a local college instead of staying at home to keep house and raise children. Though at first he and Mrs. Bagchi gravitate toward each other because they are the only Indian Americans on the tour, their relationship has progressed to the point at which they have agreed to share a hotel room on an upcoming trip to Prague.

Media Adaptations

- An unabridged audiobook of *Unaccustomed Earth* was released by Random House in 2008. The recording is narrated by Sarita Choudhury and Ajay Naidu, and the total running time is just over ten hours.

Ruma is surprised by how old her father looks when he appears, and how American, with his khakis and sneakers. Three-year-old Akash is shy of his grandfather at first, not having seen him for six months. Akash's initial bashfulness manifests itself almost as rudeness. He ignores his grandfather, but he later warms up. Ruma gives her father a tour of the house, showing him his private suite in the finished basement. She wants him to be impressed with her beautiful home, but she also feels vaguely embarrassed about the priorities it reflects. Ruma's father takes in everything with little reaction, though he is interested in the garden. He takes the teakettle outside to water some plants that are in danger of drying out and dying.

After her father unpacks his things, Ruma serves tea on the back porch. He hands out gifts—chosen by Mrs. Bagchi, although he does not mention that. He fears that Ruma would be upset if she were to learn that he has a new relationship with a woman. They discuss his most recent trip to Italy before Ruma serves dinner, an Indian feast she has spent days preparing, though she knows her cooking falls far short of her mother's. Akash turns up his nose at the food; lately, he wants only macaroni and cheese.

While Ruma is reading Akash his bedtime story, Adam calls from his business trip. He is tired and distracted, and Akash barely talks when he is put on the phone. Adam reiterates to Ruma that the decision about whether to invite her father to move in is completely hers. Ruma feels a distance from Adam, a kind of wall she blames on the fact that he has not experienced the loss of a parent as she has.

Ruma's father cleans up the kitchen, washing the dishes, putting away the leftovers, and taking out the trash. Though tired, he cannot sleep when he goes to bed. Instead he thinks about his own life when he was Ruma's age, living in a cramped apartment with a wife and two young children. Many of his Bengali acquaintances assume that he will move in with Ruma now that he is widowed, and he knows his wife would have done so without hesitation, but he is enjoying his solitary life. Part of the reason his relationship with Mrs. Bagchi works is that neither wants to marry or live with someone else. He recalls his wife's death, which was a complete surprise. Ruma cried, and he had remained stoic so that he could comfort his daughter.

The next morning Ruma wakes up to find Akash and her father in the yard. She suggests sightseeing, but her father wants to relax. Ruma feels ill-at-ease that her father seems so content, as if "her mother's death had lightened him." Once all three have eaten breakfast, they go to Akash's swimming lesson, his grandfather watching mostly through his video camera. During the drive and the lesson, Ruma and her father discuss the fact that she is not working. She claims to be happy not to have the added pressure of a job at the moment, but he is concerned that the break in her career will be hard to overcome.

Upon returning to the house, they watch the video of Akash swimming and scenes from the trip to Italy. Ruma catches sight of Mrs. Bagchi in one shot and asks about her, but her father does not use the opportunity to explain about his relationship.

Akash wakes Ruma the following morning asking about his grandfather, who is not in the house. Ruma worries until her father appears. He has driven out in search of a nursery to buy plants for the garden. Gardening seems to be the only thing he misses from his old life, now that he lives in a small condominium. As he works in the yard, he keeps Akash entertained, teaching him words in Bengali and letting him plant small toys in the soil like seeds. Ruma sees that her father enjoys Akash's company, and Akash is happy too, but still she hesitates to ask him to move in.

Ruma's father enjoys working in the garden, though he knows Ruma and Adam are unlikely to maintain all the plants once his visit is over. He wonders where the nearest post office is, because he has bought a postcard that he wants to send to Mrs. Bagchi without Ruma's knowing.

He gives Ruma detailed instructions on how to care for the garden, watering, fertilizing, and trimming. She suggests he might do it himself, making it clear that she means moving into the basement room and living there. He insists, however, that his home is back in Pennsylvania, not in Seattle. Ruma cries, disappointed.

On the last day of the visit, they decide to do a little sightseeing. As Ruma goes inside to check the boat schedule, her father is tempted by the idea of living with Akash, but he mentally confirms that staying in his own home is best for everyone.

Ruma's father leaves early the next morning before Akash is awake. He asks Ruma for a stamp so that he can mail his postcard. Though he looks everywhere, he cannot find the card where he carefully hid it or anywhere else in the room. He leaves without finding it, unhappy that the postcard has gone missing.

When Akash wakes, he asks after his grandfather and is sad to hear that he has gone home. He goes outside to play in his little garden plot, and among the toys he has planted, Ruma finds the postcard. Seeing the Bengali alphabet, Ruma understands that her father has a new romantic relationship and believes this to be the reason he does not want to move to Seattle. She puts a stamp on the postcard and puts it in the mailbox.

Characters

Adam

Adam is Ruma's husband and Akash's father. He does not appear in person in the story because he is on a business trip, though Ruma speaks to him on the telephone. Adam seems to be a supportive and open-minded person, encouraging Ruma to hire a nanny if she needs help with Akash while pregnant and leaving the decision about asking her father to move in completely up to her. Ruma, however, is not happy. She seems to resent how much Adam travels for work, yet she also feels "sometimes it was worse, not better, when Adam was home."

Akash

Akash is Ruma and Adam's three-year-old son. Like many children his age, he is sometimes stubborn, as when he refuses to eat anything other than macaroni and cheese for dinner. He is described as "a perfect synthesis of Ruma and Adam" in appearance. At first, having a child seems to fulfill Ruma. She decides to reduce her work hours so that she can spend more time at home with the baby. Then, after her mother dies, she cannot bear the idea of being away from Akash all day, so when Adam accepts a job offer in Seattle, Ruma is content to put her career on hold. However, now that she is alone with Akash so often in an unfamiliar city where she knows no one, she feels isolated—almost trapped in her role as a mother.

Mrs. Meenakshi Bagchi

Mrs. Bagchi is the widow Ruma's father meets on one of his European tours. At first, there is nothing romantic between them. They simply gravitate toward each other as the only two Bengali people on the trip. The more they see of each other, however, the more interested they become. Ruma's father knows that his relationship with Mrs. Bagchi is more about companionship than a grand passion, but they seem well suited. Neither of them wants to marry again, and both like living alone. They intend to travel together and stay in touch via email but carry on with their own lives. Mrs. Bagchi seems like a thoughtful person, helping Ruma's father shop for appropriate gifts for Ruma, Adam, and Akash, even though she has never met them.

Romi

Romi is Ruma's younger brother. He lives in New Zealand, working on a film crew. Romi does not appear directly in the story, but both Ruma and her father think about him throughout the story. Ruma seems envious of his ability to free himself from family entanglements.

Ruma

Ruma is one of the two point-of-view

characters in the story. She is a thirty-something married mother of three-year-old Akash and is expecting her second child. She is Bengali American, her parents having moved to America early in their marriage. When Ruma announced her engagement to her husband, Adam, a European American, her mother accused her of being ashamed of being Indian, but Ruma and Adam seem to have genuinely fallen in love. They have had a solid marriage for years, though moving from New York to Seattle for Adam's job, especially considering he travels so much, seems to have put a strain on their relationship. Ruma feels isolated as a stay-at-home mother, though she has happily left her job as a lawyer, not wanting to leave Akash every day after the death of her mother.

The action of the story centers on a visit to Ruma's new home in Seattle by her father. Ruma feels that she should invite him to move in, but she is afraid of taking on another responsibility when she already feels trapped in her role as homemaker and caregiver. Her father surprises her, however. He engages Akash in gardening, reads to him at bedtime, and always cleans up the dishes after supper. In addition to appreciating the material help he offers, Ruma seems to long for a family connection. Although she is hesitant to ask him to move in, when he declines, she is surprised, hurt, and disappointed. When she discovers the postcard to Mrs. Bagchi, Ruma assumes that her father wants to stay in his condo because of his new love affair, but she still sends the postcard.

Ruma's Father

Ruma's father is the other point-of-view character in the story. He is a widower of about sixty-five years. He arrives in Seattle to visit his daughter and his grandson, Akash. He seems surprised by his interest in and affection for Akash, because he was too busy working to be an involved father when his own children were growing up.

Ruma's father was shocked by his wife's unexpected death. The news still seems surreal to him. However, he has made a new independent life for himself. He is surprised to learn that he enjoys traveling. On one of his trips, he meets Mrs. Bagchi, with whom he begins a low-key romance. Ruma's father likes being retired but keeps busy with his travels and volunteer work. The only thing he seems to miss about his old life is his garden, so he works in Ruma's yard during his visit, though he is well aware that she and Adam are unlikely to tend the plants after he leaves.

Planting flowers in Ruma's garden seems partially an act of love—almost a housewarming present. It also acts as a tribute to Ruma's mother, because he plants a hydrangea, her favorite flower. He wants to keep his independence, however, so when Ruma finally asks him to move in, he explains that he is "too old now to make such a shift."

Ruma's Mother

Ruma's mother died before the main action of

the story, but she appears often in flashbacks and in the thoughts of both her daughter and her husband. She died of a bad reaction to medicine during a routine medical procedure, so her death was a surprise to everyone. Ruma had planned to take her mother on a trip for her birthday, but after her death, Ruma's father decided to take the trip on his own, sparking his travels all over Europe on organized tour trips, where he meets Mrs. Bagchi.

Ruma's parents had a steady marriage, but it was not a romantic match, like that between Ruma and Adam or Mrs. Bagchi and her late husband. Ruma assumes that her mother was mostly content with her life, but Ruma's father knows how much she disliked living in the suburbs away from the Bengali American community. She was traditional, adhering to the practice of a wife's always preparing elaborate meals for her husband and never eating until he has been fed first, but at times she resented that her husband took her hard work for granted. Fearing that her father did not pay enough attention to her mother, Ruma tried to be especially attentive to her mother's needs, always offering a listening ear.

Themes

Family

A major theme in "Unaccustomed Earth" and in most of Lahiri's work is family. Both the duties and the benefits of family ties are examined as the characters decide what to do in the next phase of their lives. Ruma has just made a cross-country move with her husband and son and is pregnant with her second child, but she is not content. Being a stay-at-home mother is not as fulfilling as she has imagined; her marriage is strained—in part because Adam travels so much, but it seems like that is not the only issue; and she feels obliged to invite her father to move in with them. Ruma is surprised to find, during her father's visit, that he is a huge help, always doing the dishes and entertaining Akash. When she finally decides to ask her father to move in, she is surprisingly hurt and disappointed that he refuses. Family obligations can be binding, but her mother's death has taught her that she will miss those ties when they are severed.

In addition to the central plot, the theme of family is echoed in many of the details of the story. For example there are several references to the trips Ruma's family took to visit family in India. Her mother and father never took any other vacations because even across continents, the pull of family is strong, whether based on love, obligation, or a combination of both. Ruma seems to share that sense of obligation to family, which is why she considers the possibility of her father's moving in with her. She feels guilty for moving away from New York, within a day's drive from her parents' home in Pennsylvania, to Seattle. Her brother, Romi, however, does not seem to feel the same restrictions. He lives in New Zealand and leads his own life, seemingly mostly separate from his family.

The family relationships Lahiri includes in "Unaccustomed Earth" are challenged by distance both physical and emotional, but the ties are unbreakable. Family will always be family. The strong bonds between family members are reflected in the physical resemblance between them: Akash is "a perfect synthesis of Ruma and Adam," and sometimes when Ruma's father looks at her, "she now resembled his wife so strongly that he could not bear to look at her directly." One cannot undo one's ties to family any more than one can change one's appearance.

Bereavement

Another central element of the story is the different ways the characters cope with bereavement. For Ruma, her mother's death seems to change almost every aspect of her life. Her marriage is affected, because she comes to resent Adam, who has never had to face the loss of a parent. Because her father makes huge changes in his life after being widowed, Ruma is forced to redefine her relationship with him. Even motherhood seems to take on a different meaning to her, especially as she faces her second pregnancy. Ruma feels trapped and isolated by suburban motherhood and wonders how her mother managed it for so long. The loss of her mother, perhaps just as much as the move to Seattle, is forcing Ruma to question her life in every respect.

In contrast, Ruma's father seems to be coping very well with the death of his wife. He decides to take her place on a trip to Europe that Ruma planned for her mother's birthday, even though Ruma herself no longer has any interest in going. Perhaps he is relieved, in part, because he has always felt that his wife resented him. Now that he is free from that feeling, he no longer wants to be entangled with the sometimes petty grievances of family life. However, by closing himself off from the negative side of those relationships, he also misses out on the positive, such as growing closer to his grandson.

The secondary characters also portray different reactions to death. Akash, because he is so young, does not understand death at all. He speaks of his grandmother's dying as if it is a great accomplishment, and he is too young to even remember her. Mrs. Bagchi provides another example of how to manage bereavement. Ruma's rather recognizes that Mrs. Bagchi has had a more romantic relationship with her late husband than he has had with his late wife. Part of Mrs. Bagchi's decision not to remarry—though her husband died after only two years of marriage, when she was still fairly young—could be that she knows she will never love another man the way she loved him. However, she, like Ruma's father, enjoys her solitary life, accomplishing things, such as teaching at a university, that she perhaps would not have done had she still been a wife or become a mother in a traditional Bengali family.

Setting

The physical setting of "Unaccustomed Earth" is central to the meaning of the story. It is significant that Seattle is a city to which Ruma's family has no previous connection. Her parents have never been there at all, a fact that emphasizes the loss Ruma feels after her mother's death. She knows that her mother will never visit and will never see the home she has made in Seattle. This is a huge difference from their being within an easy day's drive. Although Ruma's father visits, he seems to think of it as little different from his visits to foreign cities on tours. He puts down no roots, other than a connection to his grandson that he knows will fade quickly once he has left.

Topics for Further Study

- Read Kavita Daswani's 2012 young-adult novel *Lovetorn*, which portrays the struggles of Shalini, an Indian immigrant, as she tries to adjust to her new life in Los Angeles. Her life in India has been ruled by tradition, including being betrothed at the age of three. Shalini has always been content, and she genuinely cares for her fiancé—until her new friends and her first real crush force her to question everything she has known. Compare Shalini's experience with Ruma's, growing up in America and marrying a white European American man. Write a short story in which Ruma and Shalini meet. What would they talk about? What advice would Ruma offer? Use their dialogue to answer these questions.

- Using online and traditional print resources, research the Indian diaspora. To what countries have Indians most often immigrated? Investigate whether these immigrants remain and settle or return home to India. What are the most common reasons for immigrating? Create a website that includes data, maps, and links to interviews with Indian immigrants relating their experiences. Invite your classmates to visit your website and comment.

- In "Unaccustomed Earth," Lahiri explores the emotional impact of some of the decisions facing many families. Working with a group of classmates, choose one of these issues, such as inviting elderly parents to move in or professional women taking a hiatus from their careers to stay home with their young children. After researching your topic, stage a debate that highlights the advantages and disadvantages of both sides of the issue.

- Read several other stories in the collection *Unaccustomed Earth.* Pick the story you find most interesting, and write an essay comparing your chosen story with "Unaccustomed Earth." You might concentrate on the stories' themes or style, or you can focus on a specific character, comparing that character's outlook or experiences with those of Ruma or her father.

In addition to emphasizing Ruma's distance

from the family she has grown up in, the Seattle setting also increases the isolation she feels as a stay-at-home mother. Back in New York, she had other mothers of young children to talk to, but she has not made any new friends in Seattle. Ruma has also left her part-time work as a litigator, and the new house does not yet seem like a home. Ruma tells her father that she and Adam fell in love with the house, but she describes the process of furnishing the house as a careful plan. It seems almost a chore to her in her thoughts describing the house as her work now. Their home is not naturally warm and loving but a manufactured construct—it seems to be what Ruma imagines a home should be, as if one can order happiness from a catalog as easily as she picks out "sheets covered with dragons for Akash's room."

The house seems to be at a tipping point. The same could be said of Ruma's life as a whole. Her marriage to Adam and her commitment to motherhood and her career, which she has put on hold to care for Akash and her unborn child, are all in the balance. Her father works form morning until dusk on the garden, though he fears that Ruma and Adam will not care for the plants. It seems to be his effort to make the house more of a home, but he ultimately leaves it up to Ruma. Her father wants to help, but he recognizes that she is an adult now and must take responsibility for her choices. It might become a home with a well-tended garden, but it might always be a lifeless imitation of the ideal, where the plants wither for lack of water. Similarly, Ruma can choose to find a way to close the distance between her and those around her, or she can let the distance grow for lack of attention. Even though her father declines her invitation to move in, that she was willing to reach out is hopeful, giving the reader a sense that the Seattle house may turn into a true home.

Alternating Third-Person Point of View

The story is told in the third-person point of view. This means that the omniscient narrator refers to the characters as *he* or *she* instead of using *I*, as in first-person narration. Rather than stay with a single character's point of view throughout the story, Lahiri alternates between Ruma and her father. This choice gives the story great depth. Rather than seeing only one interpretation of the events of the story and the history of the family, the reader sees things from two separate points of view, which highlights the distance between the characters and the consequences of miscommunication. Because Ruma and her father have hidden so much of themselves, it is difficult for them to understand each other. Allowing the reader inside first one character's head and then the other's gives a better picture of what really happens than does a single point of view.

Multigenerational Households

The Pew Research Center defines a multigenerational household in two ways: one with two or more adult generations and one that includes both grandchildren and grandparents. The latter is sometimes referred to as a skipped-generation household, in which the grandparents raise the children and the parents do not share the residence. The number of multigenerational households in the United States has varied drastically in the last hundred years. In the early twentieth century, it was common for extended families to live together, but the percentage of US households that were multigenerational steadily declined, reaching an all-time low of 12 percent in 1980.

The recession of 2007–2009 had a huge effect on the number of multigenerational households. By the time economists declared the recession over, 51.5 million Americans (17 percent of the population) were living in such households. Even with the economy improving, however, the number of multigenerational households continued to increase, growing to 57 million (18 percent of the population) in 2012 and over 60 million (19 percent of the population) in 2014. Because the trend continued even after unemployment rates fell and Americans had more faith in the economy, social scientists began to wonder why more people were choosing to live in multigenerational households. Economic conditions were a factor, but clearly not the only one if the percentages still climbed. Some people were simply more wary—rather than extending themselves as far as financially possible, some families moved in together to save more of their earnings and to have more of a safety net if someone did lose a job. With other adults to carry the financial burden and a larger cushion in savings accounts, layoffs did not have to spell ruin.

Cultural differences play a role in the decision to form a multigenerational household. The United States is growing more ethnically and racially diverse, and Hispanic, African, and Asian Americans are more likely than white Americans to live with parents or grandparents (in 2014, 28 percent of Asian Americans, 25 percent of Hispanic Americans, and 25 percent of African Americans lived in multigenerational households, whereas this statistic was only 15 percent for white Americans). Immigration also affects the statistic, because those born in the United States are less likely to live in a household with multiple generations than are those born outside the United States.

Another recent trend is for young adults to either stay home with their parents or move back home after college or an attempt at living separately. According to the Pew Research Center, the number of younger adults (defined as between the ages of eighteen and thirty-four) "living with parents surpassed other living arrangements in 2014 for the first time in more than 130 years."

In addition to greater financial security, there are many benefits to having several generations residing in the same place. Overall, fewer people live alone, reducing social isolation, which can lead to depression, especially among older people. Cohabiting also forges stronger relationships between the generations, fostering a positive reliance on family. Children get more attention from grandparents than would be possible during occasional visits, and even the youngest children benefit from seeing the continuity of their family. Parents, often overworked with family responsibilities and earning a living, have help from adults they trust, providing everything from child care to emotional support and advice. Grandparents find new purpose and energy in helping the younger generations, especially if retirement has left them with little direction in their lives. As long as ground rules about things like privacy, finances, and housekeeping duties are discussed and respected, families can gain a greater deal from the arrangement.

The continuing trend of multigenerational households is making changes in how Americans think. Instead of being a situation people resort to only in times of financial need, it is becoming a desirable way of life for many families. There is an ongoing discussion in some states, such as California, about changing zoning laws to more easily allow separate quarters that are part of or very near the main house to allow privacy but closeness for family members such as grandparents and adult children. This is not a revolutionary concept but a traditional one. Multigenerational households were once the norm, and in many areas of the world, the practice never went out of style.

Critical Overview

Lahiri is popular with both readers and critics. The review of *Unaccustomed Earth* in *Publishers Weekly* describes the collection as stunning and continues, "Lahiri's stories of exile, identity, disappointment and maturation evince a spare and subtle mastery that has few contemporary equals." Lisa Fugard, in her review of the collection for the *Los Angeles Times*, also raves about Lahiri's talent, calling the collection powerful and Lahiri a "clear-eyed and compassionate chronicler" whose writing is "deceptively simple, its mechanics invisible, as she enters into her characters' innermost journeys," transporting "the reader into a compelling emotional landscape."

In *Short Review*, Vanessa Gebbie agrees that Lahiri's "style appears natural and effortless" and that her "prose flows by smoothly, beautifully." She singles out "Unaccustomed Earth" for particular praise among the others in the collection, marveling at the story's moments of aching poignancy as memories rise up and as Ruma and her father seek to find comfortable common ground. The story switches seamlessly between their two points of view, and between story present and memory. Lahiri explores with great tenderness what it is to be pulled in different directions in the small struggles that surface for them both each day of her father's short visit.

Liesl Schillinger, writing for the *New York Times*, points to Lahiri's mastery of characterization, pointing out how "Lahiri handles her characters without leaving any fingerprints. She allows them to grow as if unguided, as if she were accompanying them rather than training them." Lahiri uses her characterization of Ruma, Schillinger explains, to subtly illustrate her central themes: Ruma's identity, Lahiri suggests, is affected less by her coordinates on the globe than by the internal indices of her will. She is a creature of the American soil, but she carries her own emotional bearings within her.

In summing up her impressions of *Unaccustomed Earth*, Schillinger in effect describes the entire body of Lahiri's work, which often addresses issues of identity. Schillinger asserts that the collection "shows that the place to which you feel the strongest attachment isn't necessarily the country you're tied to by blood or birth: it's the place that allows you to become yourself."

What Do I Read Next?

- Lahiri won a Pulitzer Prize for her first short-story collection, *Interpreter of Maladies* (1999). Many of the volume's stories center on Indians and Indian Americans as they wrestle to reconcile their traditional heritage and life in the modern world. Family is another important theme woven through the collection.

- Sunil Bhatia's 2007 nonfiction book *American Karma: Race, Culture, and Identity in the Indian Diaspora* looks at the formation of a personal sense of identity in the Indian diaspora as a complex mixture of factors: immigration, racial attitudes, language, gender, and more.

- *Born Confused*, a 2002 young-adult novel by Tanuja Desai Hidier, tells the story of teenager Dimple Lala, who feels torn between pleasing her traditional Indian family and fitting in with her white American friends.

- Amy Tan's *The Joy Luck Club* (1989) has become a popular modern classic. The story centers on four Chinese American families, particularly on the relationships between mothers and daughters.

- Bharati Mukherjee is one of the early great writers of the Indian diaspora, paving the way for other authors, particularly women. Mukherjee is married to the Canadian American writer Clark Blaise. The couple worked together to pen *Days and Nights in Calcutta* (1977), which chronicles the year their family spent living with Mukherjee's family in Calcutta. Blaise is a fish out of water, adjusting to life in a new and unfamiliar place, and Mukherjee compares the international lifestyle she chose to what might have happened had she stayed in India.

- Kiran Sharma, the twelve-year-old protagonist of Rakesh Satyal's *Blue Boy* (2009), does not fit in anywhere. Not only is he one of the very few Indian American students in his Cincinnati school, but also he is simply different, preferring music, ballet, and dolls to basketball. Kiran's differences lead him to suspect that he is a reincarnation of the Hindu god Krishna.

Sources

Carrns, Ann, "Multigenerational Households: The Benefits, and Perils," in the *New York Times*, August 12, 2016, https://www.nytimes.com/2016/08/12/your-money/multigenerational-households-financial-advice.html (accessed September 13, 2017).

Cohn, D'Vera, and Jeffrey S. Passel, "A Record 60.6 Million Americans Live in Multigenerational Households," Pew Research Center website, August 11, 2016, http://www.pewresearch.org/fact-tank/2016/08/11/a-record-60-6-million-americans-live-in-multigenerational-households/ (accessed September 13, 2017).

Fugard, Lisa, "Divided We Love," in *Los Angeles Times*, March 30, 2008, http://articles.latimes.com/2008/mar/30/books/bk-fugard30 (accessed August 28, 2017).

Gebbie, Vanessa, Review of *Unaccustomed Earth*, in *Short Review*, http://www.theshortreview.com/reviews/JhumpaLah (accessed August 28, 2017).

Goyer, Amy, "When Generations Share Space," AARP website, September2010, http://www.aarp.org/relationships/grandparenting/in03-2009/goyer_grandparents_moving_in.html (accessed September 13, 2017).

Hawthorne, Nathaniel, "The Custom House," in *The*

Complete Works of Nathaniel Hawthorne, Vol. 5, Houghton, Mifflin, 1899, p. 27.

"Jhumpa Lahiri," in *Encyclopædia Britannica*, https://www.britannica.com/biography/JhumpaLahir (accessed August 28, 2017).

"Jhumpa Lahiri: By the Book," in *New York Times*, September 5, 2013, http://www.nytimes.com/2013/09/08/books/review/j lahiri-by-the-book.html (accessed September 13, 2017).

Lahiri, Jhumpa, "I Am, in Italian, a Tougher, Freer Writer," in *Guardian* (London, England), January 31, 2016, https://www.theguardian.com/books/2016/jan/31/jhu lahiri-in-other-words-italian-language (accessed August 28, 2017).

———, "Teach Yourself Italian," in *New Yorker*, December 7, 2015, http://www.newyorker.com/magazine/2015/12/07/te yourself-italian (accessed August 28, 2017).

———, "Unaccustomed Earth," in *Unaccustomed Earth*, Vintage Contemporaries, 2008, pp. 1–59.

Large, Jackie, and Erin Quinn, "Jhumpa Lahiri: A Brief Biography," in *The Literature &Culture of the Indian Subcontinent (South Asia)*, Postcolonial Web, http://www.postcolonialweb.org/india/literature/lahii (accessed August 28, 2017).

Review of *Unaccustomed Earth*, in *Publishers Weekly*, January 28, 2008, https://www.publishersweekly.com/978-0-307-26573-9 (accessed August 28, 2017).

Schillinger, Liesl, "American Children," in *New York Times*, April 6, 2008, http://www.nytimes.com/2008/04/06/books/review/S t.html (accessed August 28, 2017).

Witkin, Georgia, "When Families Live Together: A Survival Guide," American Grandparents Association website, http://www.grandparents.com/family-and-relationships/family-matters/when-families-live-together (accessed September 13, 2017).

Further Reading

Center, Katherine, *Everyone Is Beautiful*, Ballantine Books, 2009.

> Like Ruma in "Unaccustomed Earth," Lanie Coates, the protagonist of *Everyone Is Beautiful*, feels like she has lost her sense of self after giving up her job and moving across the country to forward her husband's career. Lanie decides to make some drastic changes that turn the family's life upside-down.

Lahiri, Jhumpa, *The Namesake*, Houghton Mifflin, 2003.

> *The Namesake* shares many themes with "Unaccustomed Earth," such as the relationships between parents and children and the immigrant experience. The story focuses on Ashoke and Ashima Ganguli as they leave Calcutta to start a new life in America, and on their son, who struggles with his identity as an American born to traditional Indian parents.

Newman, Susan, *Under One Roof Again: All Grown Up and (Re)Learning to Live Together Happily*, Lyons Press, 2010.

With college graduates returning home to live with their parents and many elderly moving in with their adult children and grandchildren, the number of multigenerational households is on the rise in America. Newman, a doctor of social psychology, examines the joys and pitfalls of this unique living situation.

Venkatraman, Padma, *Climbing the Stairs*, Putnam Juvenile, 2008.

This young-adult novel is set in Madras during World War II, when the British ruled India. As the protagonist, Vidya, seeks independence and a sense of her own identity in her grandparents' conservative, traditional household, her country struggles under colonial occupation.

Suggested Search Terms

Jhumpa Lahiri AND Unaccustomed Earth

Jhumpa Lahiri AND short stories

Jhumpa Lahiri AND Pulitzer Prize

short stories AND family relationships

working mothers OR stay-at-home mothers

multigenerational households

Indian American authors

Indian diaspora

Lightning Source UK Ltd.
Milton Keynes UK
UKHW021834290419
341804UK00026B/631/P

9 780270 527483